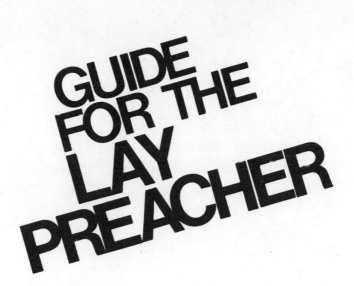

GUIDE FOR THE LAY PREACHER

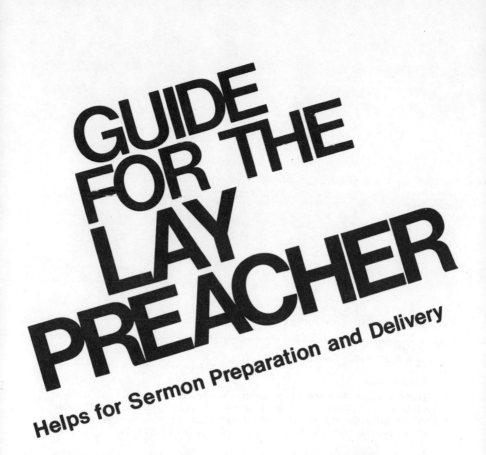

GUIDE FOR THE LAY PREACHER

Helps for Sermon Preparation and Delivery

EVAN H. BODEN

Judson Press ® Valley Forge

GUIDE FOR THE LAY PREACHER

Library of Congress Cataloging in Publication Data

Boden, Evan H.
  Guide for the lay preacher.

  1. Preaching, Lay.   I. Title.
  BV4235.L3B6   251   78-31748
  ISBN 0-8170-0836-5

The name JUDSON PRESS is registered as a trademark in the U.S. Patent Office. Printed in the U.S.A. ⊕

To my wife, Anne,
who accepts and supports me
in everything I choose to do, be it
vocation, avocation, or just for fun,
this book is dedicated, with love

Introduction

It was May 5, 1963, when I first stepped into the pulpit as a lay preacher. The place was the First Baptist Church of Johnsonburg, Pennsylvania. My pastor, Rev. Paul R. LeVan, had called me three days before and asked me if I would supply there for that Sunday. The experience was such a joy and so educational to me that I have been accepting every opportunity to supply since then.

The second most frequent church where I have supplied is my home church, the First Baptist Church of Emporium, Pennsylvania. On October 12, 1969, the Emporium church voted two other laymen and me a Certificate of License to Preach the Gospel.

The knowledge I have gained of the Scriptures in the preparation and delivery of my sermons and the many pleasant experiences I have enjoyed in supplying have prompted me to write this book. I pray that through this book many others will come to know the joy of lay preaching.

I am indebted to the churches and their congregations where I have preached and also to my wife, Anne, who typed the manuscript.

Evan H. Boden
Emporium, Pennsylvania

Contents

1
You Are Called

And how can men preach unless they are sent? As it is written, "How beautiful are the feet of those who preach good news." Romans: 10:15

Yes, "how beautiful are the feet of those who preach good news." There are very few things one can do that bring more joy, more satisfaction, and more spiritual warmth to a person's heart and soul than, as a lay person, preaching a good sermon. Therefore, if at any time you have felt even the slightest urge to preach a sermon, by all means begin to work in that direction. It is going to take time and work, but no matter how far you go, you will not count it a loss.

Now I am not going to tell you that if you work hard enough, someday you will be standing in the pulpit of a church with several hundred people in the congregation listening attentively as you finish a good sermon. That is a good ambition, a noble dream; but before we go any further, neither the call to preach nor the objective of this book is so narrowly focused. Aim for that, yes; but let the Lord say where you land. One of the greatest football coaches the game has known, Alonzo Stagg, worked and studied to be a preacher only to learn that his voice was such as to keep him from doing a good job as a preacher. He then decided he would do his preaching in a football locker room. And preach he did. Alonzo Stagg demonstrated, as many thousands have, that only some of the pulpits are at the far end of a sanctuary in a church building. I have both delivered and/or heard lay sermons beside a state park swimming pool in October addressed to an assembly of campers, at prayer breakfasts, in corporate meetings, at social parties, and in more settings than I can list here.

Only some sermons are prearranged to be delivered on Sunday at 11:00 A.M. Many are spontaneous, on-the-spot sermons given with no notice. Many more could have been given had someone been prepared. It really nags at you, at some later moment, to realize that, had you been prepared, you could have brought a short, one-sentence sermon. A scar is now on your heart for that omission.

Before someone thinks that he or she is too young to preach a lay sermon, let me say this. The first lay sermon I heard was by a high school senior in 1933, at the Calvary Baptist Church in Providence, Rhode Island. His sermon was "Where Are Your Palms on Monday?" Also, our daughter, while in high school and without even a suggestion from Mother or Father, delivered a sermon, "Disciples, Jesus Had No Other Plan."

The call to preach starts deep inside of us like a seed. The soil consists of our commitment to Jesus Christ, our desire to learn more of him, and a concerned awareness of the people around us. The breakthrough comes by way of a pastor, the deacon board, or the moderator of our church or of another church. The cultivation of the call is up to us. My sincere prayer is that this book will be one of the many tools you will use to cultivate your response to the call.

Just in case you ask yourself—or someone else asks you—why a lay person should be in the pulpit, there *are* good reasons. The most obvious reason is that there are times when the pastor of the church needs to be away on Sunday. Vacations, conventions, and extended schooling can account for six to ten Sundays out of the year. If the congregation knows that an outside speaker will supply on a given Sunday or Sundays, a large percentage of them will plan trips away on those Sundays. This has been called the "Preacher Loyalty Effect." It causes a small turnout and much embarrassment to the moderator or chairperson of the deacon board when the visiting minister sees the small turnout. The "Preacher Loyalty Effect" can be effectively reduced by putting a member of the congregation in the pulpit, a member from either your own or a neighboring church.

The not-so-obvious reasons why lay people should be in the pulpit are several. But most reasons come under one heading: some people respond better to a lay preacher than to a pastor. A psychologist could give very lengthy and detailed explanations as to why this is so. Certainly, the pastor is at a disadvantage since he or she must be there routinely every Sunday at 11:00 A.M. The pastor is saying what is expected and is paid for it. The lay persons, however, are recognized as ones who, for six days a week, walk in the same shoes as members of the congregation, at work either outside or within the house. Preaching is not their profession, but it is their confession. A confession always gathers attention. Clergy are expected to be in the pulpit. When a lay preacher is in there, it is the unexpected. And, the unexpected gets attention. When a lay person preaches a good sermon, it will be called an outstanding sermon. A pastor must preach an outstanding sermon to get a "good" rating. In other words, a lay preacher will get a rating one level above a pastor. Call it relativity if you wish.

There are some people who will try to defend their more favorable response to lay preachers by suggesting that pastors seem to talk a different language, in words and/or phraseology. I heard a sermon one time that I liked so much that I prepared a sermon along the same line. In effect, it bordered on plagiarism. After the service a young couple came to me and said, "We like to hear you preach because you tell it like it is." But it only seemed that way because I am a lay person.

If you receive the call to preach and are asked by the pastor or someone else to speak on a given date, do not refuse. Promise yourself right now not to refuse. There are two reasons why you must not refuse, and I am going to give you the second one first. Do not refuse persons who ask you, because they either know or have been told of the life you live and how it has affected others; they have been told of how you contribute in church school class or other discussions and of how you conduct yourself in the presence of others. And the first reason you cannot refuse is that you cannot refuse yourself. Since the day the seed was planted in you, there have been gathering in your mind and in your heart bits and pieces of one, two, three, or more sermons. As a maturing Christian, you cannot hold them there any longer. You must do something with them. Bring them out into daylight, arrange them this way and that way, put them into the context of your everyday life, and in a very short time your Christian life will have a whole new dimension, a new meaning, and a new orientation. Please do not destroy that call within you with such weak escapes as, "I don't know what to say," or "I'm no Bible expert."

No matter what your training or other background has been, no matter what your emotional reaction to being before an audience is, you *can* do it. The pulpit is the best place for a beginning speaker. If you have never spoken in public before, the pulpit is the best place for you to start. I have no hesitation in saying that every person in the pews before you wants you to do well. You will never have a more considerate audience than a church congregation. They are pulling for you. Some will even hear things you should have said and miss completely those errors you may make. As a lay person in the pulpit, you are not expected to be an authority or an expert. On any other platform you must have a better than average expertise, relative to the audience, on the subject. If you don't, there will be what are called sharpshooters (critics) out there, and they will attack you. Believe me, I have given speeches on mathematics, statistical analyses, electronics, and physics, and I would rather face a congregation. In short, you will never be criticized for being in the pulpit. You will be nervous, I hope, but I will discuss later how to minimize that. After you have pronounced the benediction and walked back down the aisle, you will feel totally drained, I hope. If you experience both of these conditions, you will have preached a good sermon.

What is a "good sermon"? Neither this book nor, I am sure, any other book is going to answer that question for you. The word "good" in itself is a very indefinite measure. What is good to one person may be something else to another. "Good" has no upper limit nor lower limit, and you can play all sorts of games with the term. In the case of a sermon we might well say that a "good" one might be one small influence that turns someone toward Christ; a "good" one might be a sermon that brings many people to an overt commitment to Jesus Christ. As lay people, we must work and pray for the first result, not thinking it is setting our sights too low. As I read Matthew 20:1-16, there is no "good, better, best" in the service of Jesus Christ. How, then, do we know how well we have done? Well, let us wait until we have reached that point in our study (see chapter 5).

When I began preaching as a lay person, I was very uncomfortable having what I was going to say called a sermon. It was in the bulletin:

Sermon: (Title) .... EVAN H. BODEN

That shook me. I said to myself, "I'm not a clergyman." Can you, can I, as lay persons, "preach a sermon"? It was a long time before it came from my lips that I was going to "preach a sermon." I still hesitate. But I found an answer, and the source of the answer should be used in the preparation of every sermon. We, in all of our communications, are using the English language. Most of the rules governing the use of that or any language are found in the dictionaries. Without those rules communication breaks down. My college dictionary says that to preach is to "proclaim tidings, specifically to proclaim the gospel, to deliver a sermon." Looking under "sermon," I found "a discourse delivered in public, usually by a clergyman, for the purpose of religious instruction and grounded on a passage of Scripture." Now, these two quotations from the dictionary are provided for your instruction and perhaps peace of mind, and *not* so that you can instruct some good deacon who may inform you (as one did me) that you will be speaking, not preaching. Just drop the subject and do your thing. That is what will count.

Going a little further on this matter, as lay people we must be mindful and considerate of the many traditions, interpretations, connotations and, yes, distortions that have been handed down over the years.

You frequently will find people who do not believe that a lay person can preach a sermon. And such people may not always be deacons, as I mentioned earlier. If you know of such people, tell them in advance that you will be speaking and that you respect their belief, but you hope that they will come for the singing and prayer, and leave when you start to preach. My personal experience has shown that at first they will leave, but after a few times they will stay.

In no way should you discuss the pros and cons of your being in the pulpit so that someone might equate your discussion with a disagreement. Some answers you can give might go this way: "You know, more and more lay people are stepping into the pulpit these days," or "You know, I had a problem with that point when I was first asked, and I learned that a sermon is a speech based on a passage of Scripture, and I have selected a passage of Scripture for my sermon." If they then ask where you got this idea, just say, "Mr. Webster." Other escape lines are: "Many people think that way," or "To some, that is traditional," or "It's a matter of semantics." But again, don't get into a debate over it or be involved in anything that might be construed to be an argument. It will harm not only your efforts but also the efforts of those who will follow. And, by the way, this is one of the areas where you have a responsibility to those who will follow you.

PREPARATION

"If anyone purifies himself from what is ignoble, then he will be a vessel for noble use, consecrated and useful to the master of the house, ready for any good work" (2 Timothy 2:21).

In this part of the chapter, more than in the others, I am going to use an analogy. As you know, analogies are very effective teaching tools, and you, too, will be using them. Because I am an avid football fan, I will use that sport for my analogy. One can draw a distinct parallel between preparing oneself to play football and preparing oneself to be a lay preacher. Certainly one must have a good and healthy body even to consider playing football. So, too, one must have a good and strong spirit to be a lay preacher. To play football, one must have a commitment to the game; to lay preach, one must have a commitment to Jesus Christ, the Son of God. At no lesser point can the football player—or you—start. So here we start.

The player will study the rules, techniques, signs, and signals. So will you. The football player will observe by watching films of games. You will observe your own pastor and other pastors. Then comes lifting weights and practice. To develop your preaching strength and ability, you will "lift weights" and "practice."

These are not sequential steps of preparation for the player or for you. Preparation for lay preaching is an all-out program. So, I am going to give you a four-part program, and you should carry the four parts out concurrently.

1. Study Biblical Sermons—If you are going to preach a sermon, you must make a study of sermons. I wish that I could say that this point is so obvious that everyone does it. I am afraid not. Begin your study of sermons in the Bible.

The first sermon we think of in the Bible is the Sermon on the Mount. Unfortunately, the Sermon on the Mount is not a sermon but rather the teachings of Jesus on the meaning of obedience. The Sermon on the Mount is more of a collection of sermon themes. Therefore, when you are at the point where you have a topic and you are in the research phase, look to the Sermon on the Mount.

The sermon by Paul to the church at Antioch of Pisidia,

recorded in Acts 13:16-41, is considered the model sermon. The question of whether Paul actually wrote it or Luke rewrote it is not important to you in your study. As we have it, it is a model sermon. Therefore, here is the first sermon you should study. First, read the sermon through several times. Then put a box on a table as an improvised lectern, stand up and give the sermon as though it were your own. Do it again and again until you really feel it.

The next step is to outline Paul's sermon. Outline it just as you were taught to do in high school English class. I always hated to write outlines in school. Since then I have learned of the importance and usefulness of an outline. Most of the time now an outline is all I put on paper when preparing a sermon.

Now study the outline. After you have done this, I am sure you can see how the sermon has continuity, how it traces the hand of God from Moses to God's risen Son, and how Paul lifts his audience away from David, who saw corruption, into the saving grace of Jesus Christ, who saw no corruption. After you have studied the outline, go to your Bible and a short concordance and search out some of Paul's source material. With the outline and the source material write a sermon. After you have finished, compare your version with Paul's.

This same study procedure can be used on the other two sermons by Paul in Acts 17:22-31 and Acts 26:2-23. These last two sermons by Paul are what I call "sprint" sermons, again using the football analogy. Paul was suddenly in two situations where he could deliver a sermon. In one case, he was defending his life. There were no hymns or Scripture reading before the sermon. The time was now—bang!— and Paul responded. You will have your day, and maybe when you are finished, you will have a warm smile inside, as I am sure Paul did in front of Agrippa, having gotten a lick in for the Lord.

I join with those who classify the first three Gospel accounts as Synoptic, and John as the preacher's preacher. I like John; I like his style. Take a moment from your reading here and look at the Gospel of John. For example, look at the third chapter. Jesus is talking with Nicodemus, and John gives an account of that meeting up through the fifteenth verse. In the next six verses John gives us a sermon. In the same chapter John, beginning with the twenty-second verse, is again giving an account and by verse thirty-one he is back in the pulpit. Come to think of it, that is just what Paul did at Antioch.

2. Study Contemporary Sermons—Now start looking at contemporary sermons. Frequently, when you hear a sermon on the radio or television, there also will be an offer of copies at a small price. If you cannot obtain a copy, with a little practice you can make a rough outline as the preacher talks. Your library may have books of sermons. With each of these sermons do as you did with Paul's sermon at Antioch. Don't do too many sermons by one person, or you will end up sounding like that person. On the other hand, if you really want to sound like a certain preacher, then concentrate on that one person's sermons. I read that Benjamin Franklin practiced his favorite writer's style so that it would become his own.

I am sure that by this time you are wondering why I am not giving you long lists of books to read on the subject. Frankly, I was unable to find books appropriate for you to use at this point. To those who have written books on preparing one for lay preaching, I must apologize. Yes, there are books on public speaking and homiletics; these are courses you may want to take after you have had a few experiences of preaching.

3. Observe Speakers—In the first part of this chapter I have told you to study sermons. Now I am going to have you go further with the sermons you witness in church or on television. Observe the speakers; this includes body language and speaking style. How do they walk up to the lectern? Do they begin with a pause to get attention? What kind of body language do they have? What is their timing?

If you really like the sermons of your pastor, take notes. You might be self-conscious about this, so if you are righthanded, sit to the far right and fairly forward in the church, lefties on the other side. This way, fewer people will notice what you are doing because they will be looking the other direction, and it will be difficult for them to read what you are writing.

4. Practice Speechmaking—Now comes the "weight lifting" and "sprints." When you are alone in a room or driving someplace alone, make a speech. Speak on any subject, the more spontaneous the better. Open up a magazine, turn on a radio and find a talk show; somehow, find a subject and make a speech. The subject matter is not important. It is like lifting weights—to your arm muscles, it makes no difference if you are lifting one hundred pounds of sugar or one hundred pounds of iron. This "weight lifting" develops your ability to think and talk on your feet. As you get further along, begin to develop a sense of how long twenty minutes is. You don't need to buy a stopwatch. Find an old clock or watch, set it on the hour and speak until twenty minutes are past. It won't be long until people will be able to set their watches by you. I don't like to see speakers looking at their watches. I know immediately that they don't have a real handle on what they are going to say. My confidence is shaken.

Collecting Material

Yes, you are going to preach. And you are going to need material. Like a storekeeper, you have to start putting some things on the shelf. So get some three-by-five-inch file cards and a few file folders and begin collecting. Collect anything and everything that strikes a chord in you. Don't make any judgments on them; just put them in the file. At most you will use 20 or 30 percent of them, so you are going to need a lot of them. Unfortunately, you don't know what you are going to preach on in the future, so you can't make any premature decisions on which to keep. As your file begins to fill and you are preaching, that file is going to give you everything from a sermon theme to a missing link in a sermon chain.

Between the reading of the end of this chapter and beginning of the next, do some very prayerful thinking about your decision to preach. Not that you might make a decision not to go ahead with your plan; no, but you must be sure that your feet are on the ground and that you are in control of your preparation and your thinking. I am confident that you will go ahead and that you are ready to take the next step. The next step is to sit down with your pastor, the church moderator, and the chairman of the deacon board. Tell them what you have been doing and that you want to supply at your or any other church. When a minister knows that he or she is going to be away on a given Sunday, the minister will contact other pastors in the area for possible supply. After you do this, start putting together a sermon. You may get called as soon or sooner than I was. I walked in the door at 11:30 at night from a business trip that had taken me to Chicago, San Francisco, Dallas, Chicago, and home. The telephone was ringing. Putting down my briefcase and suitcase, I answered the telephone. It was my pastor, and he began by reminding me of my interest in supplying and told me that a church thirty miles away needed someone that coming Sunday. After I told him where I had just been, he said he would call someone else. I said, "No, I promised myself and I will do it."

Short notice has its advantage; there's no time to get nervous. It is like my first solo flight in an airplane; my instructor said, "I'm getting out. You go around twice by yourself." If the people know you are there on short notice, they love you for stepping in at the last moment. I was asked one Sunday morning between church school and church. It works out.

The purpose of this chapter has been to encourage and help prepare those of you who have a sincere desire in your heart to preach. It is right for you to desire to preach. The voice within you calling you to stand up and be heard for the Lord is a true voice and will continue to speak to you as you prepare and as you deliver your sermon.

Jesus said to Pilate (John 18:37*b*), "Everyone who is of the truth hears my voice." You who would preach, listen.

2

Selecting Your Topic

"Brethren, if you have any word of exhortation for the people, say it."   Acts 13:15*b*

There is another title for this chapter, but it is so common that I decided not to use it. Let's call it a subtitle: "What Am I Going to Say?" Well, the answer to that question is a lot closer to being easy than difficult. How do I know this without knowing you personally? Well, for one thing, you are reading chapter 2 of this book, and, whether you know it or not, you have things inside of you that want to be said which have caused you to open this book and have kept you reading this far. If this is not true, then you *do* have a question. And that question is: Why am I considering lay preaching? Saying it another way, you don't know how much you know and can say on a subject until you sit down and start writing. If you put it on paper, you can measure it. Someone once said, "To measure is to know." If someone were to ask you what the square of "pi" (3.1416) is, you would say, "I don't know." And so would I. However, both of us know we can take paper and pencil (or an electronic calculator) and multiply the number by itself and get the answer 9.8696 (I used a calculator). So the only answer that you should give to the question of this chapter is "I don't know; I'll have to give it some prayer and some thought." Any other answer will get you in trouble.

Paul was an experienced speaker, both in the role of an enemy to Christians and later in that of an apostle. He had studied Jesus Christ while he was in both roles. He had witnessed the power of Jesus Christ in himself and those he met in both roles. He was accustomed to being called on to speak. What is more, he desired to be called on. So when the rulers of the synagogue called on him to speak, we read, "So Paul stood up, and motioning with his hand said . . ." (Acts 13:16). Paul's topic was the simple Good News of Jesus Christ.

Speakers in the time of Paul were few and far between; the people did not have copies of the Scriptures to read for themselves, and the social pressures of everyday life were simple. Today's congregation has heard many speakers in church, radio, and television; members have Bibles of their own, most have attended church school, and the everyday social pressures are complex. Therefore, sermon topic selection requires greater work, particularly for the new speaker.

BASIC RULES OF TOPIC SELECTION

Virtually everything starts with ground rules. If the rules are good and they are obeyed, the result will be good. I have three ground rules which I use, and I like to think they have served me well.

Rule One: Select your own topic. If it is going to be your sermon, then it must begin with your own topic. So don't let anyone tell you what your subject will be. When someone gives you a topic to speak on, several things take place.

First, the work and time required to prepare a sermon on that topic will be increased tenfold. The odds are very high that the topic will draw a blank in your thinking and experience. You will frequently ask yourself, "What did 'he' have in mind when 'he' gave me the topic? Am I going to meet 'his' objective?" The sermon will be oriented to "him" and not to your audience. Another thing (and perhaps worst of all), the topic title might tell you what you are going to say, and it may be contrary to your own beliefs. It can't happen? Watch. Some years ago I was asked by the ministerium in our town to speak one night in the Week of Prayer. I was given the title "Unanswered Prayer." I opened the sermon by reading the title as printed in the Week of Prayer bulletin, and then I gave the subtitle "Mission Impossible." I don't happen to believe that there are unanswered prayers, just unanswered instructions, demands, and the like.

When you select your own text, it will be accompanied by those ingredients of which good sermons are made: thoughts that have lived within you; experiences which have left a deep and lasting impression on your heart and your mind; books, articles, and Scriptures you have read; sermons and speeches you have heard; and quotations that have warmed your heart. They are there in your memory bank, and they will come forward as you begin to "feel" a topic.

Now and then, people, including young people, come to me for advice. I always say that I never give advice for two reasons. If the advice leads to failure, I don't want to be blamed for it; and if it leads to success, I want the person to feel good all over for what he or she has accomplished. After all, success or failure of a decision is largely a function of how the decision was implemented. If, as I am confident it will be, your sermon is a good one, the warmth and glow that you will feel in your own heart is all yours—yours to share with the Lord, not some third party.

Before concluding with this rule, I must point out that there is no conflict between selecting your own sermon topic and sermons preached on a seasonal theme. On the contrary, as a mature Christian you cannot have partaken of seasons like Christmas and Easter without interpreting them to yourself. Your interpretations are unique and, as such, will be valuable to others as they establish, develop, or remold their interpretations.

Rule Two: Base your sermon on a passage of Scripture. The natural reaction of a lay person is to shy away from a scriptural message. That is not only wrong, but, as I see it, it can't be done. Why? There are two reasons. First, the common dictionary defines a sermon as a speech based on a passage of Scripture. Secondly, in the words of George Buttrick, "There is no true preaching except biblical preaching. . . ."[1] As I see it, Mr. Buttrick's article should be required reading for all who would step into the pulpit of a church. Mr. Buttrick leaves no doubt that there is, as he says, "a blood bond between the Bible and preaching."[2] He attacks those who use the new

---

[1] George A. Buttrick, "The Bible and Preaching," *The Interpreter's One-Volume Commentary on the Bible,* ed. Charles M. Laymon (Nashville: Abingdon Press, 1971), p. 1255.
[2] *Ibid.*

psychology, the new science, the new drama, or a four-cent (now twenty-cent) newspaper as a base for a sermon. I am a scientist by education and profession, and many is the time I have had to sit and listen to preachers trying to make a sermon of what they think science says. A few times, when going out, I have wanted to shake their heads, not their hands. I am certain that experts in other fields have had the same experience. So you see, if you take a nonbiblical basis, you are going to get arguments. You may not know about the arguments, but they will exist.

You can preach a Bible sermon. Why? Because God planned it that way in the parables, miracles, and discourses of Jesus. Each time someone preaches on a passage of Scripture, God the Father and Jesus Christ are reflected in a different way to very many, very different people. Each time a passage of Scripture is used as the base of a sermon, some will be introduced to that passage; for the first time some will receive a new understanding, some a new perspective, some an amplified understanding, and some a confirmation of the understanding they have held for a long time. That is Christian growth.

When I began preaching lay sermons, I decided that there were certain passages I would avoid. I foolishly called them, "Safe-harbor passages for lay people." The prodigal son and the good Samaritan are examples. My reason was not that I had heard so many sermons on those passages that they bored me; on the contrary, I'll be all ears the next time and every next time someone preaches on them. I just thought they weren't challenging enough. I was wrong. Ten years after that decision, I preached on the good Samaritan and the reaction I got would put that sermon in my top ten.

Yes, you can preach a Bible sermon. And to find a topic, just open your Bible and let it use you. When you turn the pages of your Bible, I sincerely hope you will find words, sentences, and whole passages underlined, and words or question marks in the margins— even clippings between the pages. I have so many things in my Bible that it looks like a lawyer's file drawer. A few times I have conducted Sunday worship services for sectional camp-ins of the National Campers' and Hikers' Association. If I didn't put elastic bands around the sections of my Bible which I am not using, with one gust of wind I would become a "litterbug."

Your occupation or other interests may lead you to draw from one of those areas, thinking you will do better on home ground. True,

67257

you may, but do it on home ground, not in the pulpit. The best witness that you can give for Jesus Christ as an industrialist, scientist, steelworker, lawyer, sports star, or whatever, is to preach from the Bible. One or maybe two illustrations from your field may be acceptable. Beyond that point the risk is too great that you will draw the attention of the listeners away from the Bible and your witness, and toward your position and your ability in that field. And that is not why you are there. It is right and proper for your audience to know your profession and/or your discipline, but make that known during the announcements; don't rob your preaching time or your congregation's attention when you inform them.

Don't get me wrong—your job and recreational experiences can be seasoning to a sermon. But they are not the kind of seasonings that go in every kettle. In some instances, it serves well to bring one's profession or recreational activity into a sermon, though lightly, to show that there is no conflict between the person in the pulpit and the person at work or at play.

By now you are pounding this book and asking, "What is wrong with drawing from work and sports experiences?" The answer is "Nothing." *But,* there are many traps and pits into which you may fall. Let me list some of these pits, starting with one already given:

1. You may give a shop-based "sermon" and not a Bible-based one. I am not saying that there is a sharp line beyond which your speech becomes shop talk. With me, it would be fairly sharp. Each listener will draw the line in a different place, and there is the start of the problem.

2. The focus comes on you and what you are and not on Jesus Christ and what he is. Some of your listeners will hint to themselves and others that you are showing yourself off. In like manner, some will dismiss the whole sermon with, "I don't care what's going on over at that plant." You run the risk of dividing your audience. Among those whom you will lose are some of your co-workers. "I work there all week and I don't want to hear someone make a sermon of it."

3. Technical terms and language will infiltrate your message. People will lean to their neighbor in the pew and question, "What's a _____?"

"Are there exceptions?" you ask. I don't know how there could be, and I don't like the thought that there might be. Just think of the impact of an NFL football hero—the most valuable player in the

Super Bowl, we'll say—preaching a truly biblical sermon, not once using words like "teammate," "forward pass," or "inside handoff."

Rule Three: Be positive. It will seem to you that this rule is premature and should be in the next chapter. Not so. The topic you select and the title you give it will dictate the orientation of your sermon. "Why should I always be positive? Our pastor is not always positive," you comment. The answer is in your question; he or she, as the pastor, has certain responsibilities which you don't have as a guest preacher. What is more, it may be necessary now and then for him or her to dip into the negative, but, on the average, the pastor must be positive. Also, it may be that you did not recognize the positive as well as the negative in the sermon.

There are two good reasons for you to want to be positive. First of all, the Word of God is a cheerful word. *Gospel* means "*Good News*." The gospel of Jesus Christ is *positive*. The image of God in us enables us to create and to build. That is positive. Jesus said, "I came that they may have life, and have it abundantly" (John 10:10). That is *positive*. Paul was told by the rulers of the synagogue, ". . . Men and brothers, if you have any message of encouragement for the people, by all means speak" (Acts 13:15, J. B. Phillips). That is positive. In other words, if they had an ax to grind or if they came to boast or complain, they were to remain seated and silent. Paul in no way took exception to the conditions of the invitation. "So Paul stood up, and motioning with his hand said . . ." (Acts 13:16). It is likewise enjoined upon you, if you have words of encouragement, by all means speak. If, on the other hand, you come with an ax to grind, to boast, or to complain, then hire a hall and make a speech. Believe me, it is very easy to slip into one of those ruts. So let that "hand-slap for doing nothing" make you more cautious.

The second reason for a positive approach in your sermon is that more people will pay attention to a positive sermon than to one lambasting this or that. Almost one hundred years ago, Eugene Field said, "Put not your trust in vinegar—molasses catches flies." There is another word from a sage that applies here. It is from Paul's letter to the Galatians (6:7), ". . . for whatever a man sows, that he will also reap." If your sermon is positive, then your efforts will be judged in a positive climate. I think that is what you will want.

METHODS OF TOPIC SELECTION

So much for the ground rules. Now we can get down to the meat and potatoes of selecting a topic. However, first let me reveal a hang-up I have. I take a dim view of people who use what I call the "drop and pop" method. "I just opened my Bible and the Lord told me to preach on what was there." In other words, they drop their Bible and pour out the cerebral popcorn. No, I believe the Lord wants us to do our homework with a capital *W*.

As I mentioned before, sit down with your Bible, preferably in a comfortable chair and in quiet. I take my Bible and hold it up in front of me, closed between my two hands. And, after a moment of quiet listening, I say aloud in a prayerful tone, "Well, Bible, *we* must find a subject to speak on." I then open it and begin turning the pages. I talk to myself about the passages I see. Sometimes I reflect on sermons I have heard on this or that passage. This may go on for thirty minutes or three hours. On a few occasions I have had to repeat this procedure the next evening. This time it is seldom more than an hour. If you do this, finally you will find a word, a name, a phrase, a sentence, or a chapter, that stirs something in you, and the wheels begin to move.

At this point you move to a desk and begin taking notes. For starters, let us say that it is a word that struck some resonance in your thinking. Let me show you how this can work.

Specific Words

1. You find interest in the trial of Jesus. You are reading in the eighteenth chapter of John. Near the end of that chapter you find Pilate asking what truth is. That is interesting because he said, "What is truth?" not "What is *the* truth?" Was Pilate poking fun at Jesus, as so many sermons say; or was he asking a very intellectual question? Notice that he didn't wait for an answer. You turn to your concordance and find many references under "truth." You will find that most of them are in John's account of the gospel. You may learn along the line that John's is known as the "truth gospel." The topic is now thickening. If you go to a library, you will find that Pilate's question has confounded people for thousands of years before and since Pilate asked Jesus that question. Now your problem is not "What am I going to say?" but "How can I do it in twenty minutes?"

2. You are reading in Second Corinthians in the third chapter. Your eyes stop on "letter of recommendation." What is this—they had *them* then? Did you ever write a letter of recommendation for someone candidating for acceptance in a school or a position in a firm? What did you put in it? If, as Paul says, we are letters of

recommendation for Jesus Christ, what is in "them"? Jesus is a candidate seeking to be accepted. Wasn't Jesus just such a letter from God the Father? Consult a book on letter writing, checking the section on "Letters of Recommendation."

3. In John 3:3 you find the phrase "born anew." "Born again" is a term we are hearing a lot these days. Maybe it is time to review what it means. How often does it appear elsewhere in the Bible? Only in First Peter, according to my concordance. If that is all, then it is not important. But Jesus said it. Ah! *That* is important. What does it mean? Well, he said it to a well-educated man. That means it has a deep and profound meaning.

A footnote in my Bible says, "from above," as another translation of the term. My dictionary says "anew" means for an additional time, afresh, or in a new form. What about the word "borne", past participle of "bear"? Try your dictionary on that word. Maybe Jesus did mean born as in birth, the beginning of life. Maybe we have an unborn spirit in ourselves. If that is the case, then with that birth there would be an infant that would grow through adolescence to maturity—not a poor line of reasoning!

In the above examples, do you see the kind of detective work that goes on in preparing a sermon? At the risk that you might think I am exaggerating, I get excited as the trail begins to warm. Now, let us see what we do with a name.

Names

1. *Thomas,* the twin, the doubter. What was he really like? Was he really the only one who had doubts, or was he the catchall for a condition that others had then and millions and millions of people have had since then? Aren't there thousands of Thomases standing outside your very church door? Was he weak or was he strong? Was he loyal and dedicated? Would you like to be like him? The answer you give to that last question may be interesting even to you. You're limited to the book of John for your information; however, John gives us a good picture. Thomas may have a negative identification in the Bible, but, as I see him, he is a towering "plus."

2. *Gideon,* in Judges 7. Vision was required of the Lord to call Gideon to lead an army. He said, "Hey, I want proof that you are the Lord." Once he knew, though, he signed up thirty-two thousand for his army. What is more, he was still standing there to lead the army that had been whittled down to three hundred. What strength—what

resourcefulness! The first cut in the thirty-two thousand is not too hard to understand. But why the next? What difference does it make how a soldier drinks water in the field? You may have to ask a good woodsman to answer that. When you learn, you will say, "Of course!" Maybe that is why Jesus had twelve disciples, not twelve hundred.

3. *Nehemiah.* Here was a giant when the Lord needed a giant to rebuild the wall. This is a fabulous story—how Nehemiah wrestled with himself, how he planned, how he responded to threats of danger, and how he kept the law of the Lord. If we would plan and execute as Nehemiah did, we, too, would be Nehemiahs.

There are many interesting Thomases, Gideons, and Nehemiahs in the Bible. To get a quick look at some of them, look at Frank S. Mead's book *Who's Who in the Bible.* He has short, thumbnail sketches on two hundred fifty people in the Bible. Pick out the seldom-studied people and those who personify people we meet and work with day in and day out.

Phrases and Sentences

Here is another avenue I like to follow: a phrase or a sentence. See what you can do with three of these.

1. At the time of the writing of this chapter, I am collecting material for a sermon which will use 1 John 3:18 for its theme: "Little children, let us not love in word or speech but in deed and in truth." Do you see how that verse is the bottom line of what is called the "love chapter," 1 Corinthians 13? To love by word or speech is to give lip service to the law. We are not under the law when we are in Christ. Paul here is sounding like James in James 1:22. By the way, if you want a "love chapter," read from that verse through to the end of chapter 4.

2. There will be times, as you go on as a lay preacher, when you will find a sentence or a phrase that will leap out at you. You may have never heard a sermon or even a church school lesson on that sentence, but, because of a unique combination of events and readings, there it is. The following example is just such a sentence. As I recall, my attention fell on it after I had been deer hunting and had gathered sticks to build a fire. I carried a can of stew in my coat and heated it for lunch. "Paul had gathered a bundle of sticks and put them on the fire . . ." (Acts 28:3). Use symbolism here. The sticks can be the word of God, interactions with other Christians, or what you have done for those who have not accepted Jesus Christ. The fire?

The results of putting those sticks on the fire is the added warmth to the body and to the spirit. Warmth is added to the spirit of Jesus Christ in those whom we touch. Touch? Touched by what? Touched by fire. There is a book with a similar title.

For my third example, here is a sentence or a phrase that integrates Christian principles.

3. Second Corinthians 5:18: "All this is from God, who through Christ reconciled us to himself and gave us the ministry of reconciliation." If it were not for the magnitude of this sentence, we could have picked out the key word "reconcile" and proceeded as we did earlier. However, to do so would be to take the word out of context. The context is an equilateral triangle of God, Jesus Christ, and reconciliation. Don't let this stop you from consulting a dictionary for a meaning of the word reconciliation. We must understand the parts of this triangle. My dictionary says that it means to restore to friendship, harmony, or communion.

Parallel Situations

At this point I would like to talk to you about parallels of then and now. Compare the customs, practices, people, and groups that we find in the Bible with those we experience now. If you start looking for these parallels, you will be surprised to learn how many more there are than you thought. Here is a favorite of mine:

1. John 9:21b. ". . . Ask him; he is of age, he will speak for himself." A man had been blind since birth. Jesus had given him sight. Try this situation on yourself. You have a son, born blind, and now some doctor gives him full sight. Will the joy in your heart be so limited that your answer would be the same? Doesn't their answer sound like, "We don't want to get involved"?

2. Judges 9:7-15, KJV. And when they told it to Jotham, he went and stood in the top of Mount Gerizim, and lifted up his voice, and cried, and said unto them, Hearken unto me, ye men of Shechem, that God may hearken unto you. The trees went forth on a time to anoint a king over them; and they said unto the olive tree, Reign thou over us. But the olive tree said unto them, Should I leave my fatness, wherewith by me they honour God and man, and go to be promoted over the trees? And the trees said to the fig tree, Come thou, and reign over us. But the fig tree said unto them, Should I forsake my sweetness, and my good

fruit, and go to be promoted over the trees? Then said the trees unto the vine, Come thou, and reign over us. And the vine said unto them, Should I leave my wine which cheereth God and man, and go to be promoted over the trees? Then said all the trees unto the bramble, Come thou, and reign over us. And the bramble said unto the trees, If in truth ye anoint me king over you, then come and put your trust in my shadow: and if not, let fire come out of the bramble, and devour the cedars of Lebanon.

This is an Old Testament fable. I don't think any two people could preach the same sermon here. If you change the "characters" and the excuses to your present-day experiences, you can have a ball. The strange thing is, I don't recall ever hearing a sermon on the passage.

3. John 12:13; 19:6; 18:40. "They . . . went out to meet him, crying, 'Hosanna! Blessed is he who comes in the name of the Lord.'" "Crucify him, crucify him!" "Not this man, but Barabbas!" This happened during the week that Christ died. Those people haven't died; they are still with us. Their cry is the same. It is still being heard in our streets, our courts, our politics, and yes, even in our churches.

Passages You Have Not Understood

Have you ever read a passage of Scripture that caught your interest and then said to you, "I defy you to understand me"? Well, this has happened to me several times. The only thing I can do is stay with it and solve the problem. I strongly advise you to do likewise. When you solve it—and you will—you will feel so good that giving the sermon will almost become incidental. Also, when you master the passage, there is little added work to assembling the sermon. I can make that last statement for two reasons. First, you will have read it so many times, done so much research on it, and talked to yourself so much about it that you could speak on it at the drop of a hat. Second, if you keep a running record of your progress while working on that passage, you will have your outline all prepared. You can even start your sermon by saying, "I have been working for four weeks on the Scripture that was read earlier, and I still can't figure it all out. I am caught between. . . ." It is a very effective technique. It has worked on me and for me. The first time I heard this done was about thirty years ago at a physics honorary banquet. The speaker was five feet five inches in stature; but when he spoke, he was six feet six inches. Let me give you one example and how I worked it out.

Lay this book down and read John 10:1-21. My first reaction was that Jesus was telling us that there were crooks running around. "Now wait a minute," I thought. "It can't be that simple because Jesus gave it, John reported it, and it is the only parable that John reported. There is something of deep meaning here." I consulted three commentaries, and they slipped over it as if it were not there. The Gospel of John is my favorite book, and, to me, John wrote lean meat and potatoes. So I sat down and wrote out my understanding at that point. A few days later I read it again and made notes. This time, though, it was before breakfast. The next time it was after lunch, then again before dinner. Early in my search I recognized that those twenty-one verses belonged with the ninth chapter, and I decided that was why the Jews were so upset about what Jesus said. I still made notes. I stood up, read it out loud, and before I finished the fifth verse, I had it.

His voice—there it is—what about his voice? The sheep, his sheep, will know the voice of the Good Shepherd. Who is the Good Shepherd? He is the Shepherd who is not a hireling and, therefore, who owns the sheep. They are his sheep; so he will lay down his life for them. He is Jesus Christ. What is the message? The message is that if we don't know his voice, we don't know when he calls us. Or we may follow the voice of strangers. How do we get to know his voice? It is in the Bible; listen to it every day. Then you will know his voice.

What do I have now? Here are my notes on this whole sequence:

A nice nursery story.
Should be in chapter 9.
Robbers don't come in by the door.
The Good Shepherd is not a hireling.
The sheep know his voice.
To be his sheep, we must know his voice.
We should flee from those whose voices we do not know.
Jesus is the Good Shepherd.
He *laid* down his life for his sheep.
There are other sheep to come into that fold.
We must learn his voice; but how?
Listen to it in the Bible.

Thirty minutes more work gave me an outline ready to take into the pulpit.

In the above examples, I have tried to show you the various

mechanics that may be employed to find a topic—a topic with enough support material that will allow you to make the clear decision that you are ready to put it together.

3
Research
and Assembly

"**Ask, and it will be given you; seek, and you will find; knock, and it will be opened to you.**" Matthew 7:7

"**Paul had gathered a bundle of sticks and put them on the fire.**" Acts 28:3

One frequent analysis of a poor speech is: "He didn't do his homework." In other words, the speaker did not fully research the material used or the words used. Don't let an inadequately researched subject or reference destroy your effort. Be sure that you know the various meanings and connotations of every word you use.

RESEARCH

This section of the chapter may be described as "how to implement Matthew 7:7." Because you are going to ask questions about your subject, you are going to seek everything available to you on your subject, and you are going to knock on many doors. The doors that you knock on are front covers of books and doors to introductions, analogies, illustrations, and so on.

In chapter 1, I said that you should start collecting thoughts. The first step in research is to go to that collection of thoughts and see what you have found on the subject. It is here that you may find another reason why you selected the subject that you did. The subject has been in your thinking longer than you realized. Or you may find that this is a new subject and that your collection of thoughts is of little or no help.

Let me say a little more about collecting clippings and thoughts. If you are a very systematic person (which I am not), you may want to start a card file using three-by-five or five-by-eight-inch cards. Or you may use several shorthand notebooks labeled by topic. Unfortunately, notebook notes don't have the mobility that cards have. You can copy from them, however, and the notes don't get lost. If you are a natural-born collector as I am, envelopes, file folders, and boxes will collect more items than any systematic filing system. They receive and hold clippings, notes, and scraps of paper made in a business meeting or a thought jotted on the corner of a church bulletin. I don't always get them in the right file folder, but when I find misfiled ones, I toss them in the right file folder.

All right, you have a sermon topic and your "collection." Where do you go from here? To start with, take a felt marker and a large piece of paper and make a sign of your subject. Lay that sign on the floor where you can see it, or with masking tape, tape it on the wall. I use the floor for reasons that you will soon see. Take another piece of paper, and make a sign that states your objective. Place this sign to the right and below your subject sign. You now have visible signs to guide your preparation. One sign, your subject, says what you are going to talk about; and another, your objective, says what you want to accomplish with your subject. For example, your subject may be Thomas, the doubter. Your objective is to show that Thomas was not alone and that there are millions of Thomases outside of our churches today. With subject and objective in sight, dig into your collection of notes and clippings. Those that you find which you *might* use, place in a left-to-right sequence. Please note that I have emphasized "might." Some years ago I took a two-week course in decision making. The course was called "Problem Solving," but the methods they taught for solving problems are equally effective in any kind of decision making. You have a problem of deciding what you are going to say and what you are not going to say. In the course I took, we were taught to collect as many ideas as we could which in any way were connected to the problem. Most important, we were to make no decision on those ideas until they were all together. The next step was to review each idea and determine how it related to the total picture. At this point the ideas were graded and eliminated from the bottom up. Likewise, you are going to lay out every clipping or thought that *might* relate to your subject and objective. Make no decision beyond that point, because the only decision you have made thus far is on your subject and your objective. As you lay these items in place, you are assembling a picture of your sermon. It is patchy, but it is a picture.

While you are doing this—you are keeping one eye on your subject and one eye on your objective—thoughts will come to you. Write them on pieces of paper or cards and put them into the picture.

Now it is time to "hit the books." To do so sooner might result in a premature decision based on earlier thoughts you had on the subject. To "hit the books" does not mean to go charging into a library. You are preparing a lay sermon, not a thesis for a Doctor of Theology degree. Until you learn to swim and swim well, don't go charging into deep water. Stay in shallow water with a few good and well-accepted books.

Obviously, the Bible is the starting point. Until you are more skilled and aware of words whose meanings have changed, use a newer translation. You will find it helpful to have two translations. If a paraphrased version helps your understanding, all well and good. However, do not quote from a paraphrase version as a translation. Read the passages relating to the subject of your sermon each time you sit down to work. Follow up every cross reference. Sometimes they will lead you to a better passage for your subject than you had earlier.

A concordance of the size found in the back of some Bibles is adequate for your first one hundred sermons. Also, you will need a commentary. *Halley's Bible Handbook* will meet your needs for the first ten or fifteen sermons, after which you will want to step up to a commentary like *The Interpreter's One-Volume Commentary on the Bible* by Abingdon Press, a very good investment. It also has forty-three very informative articles and sixteen maps.

If you are going to preach on one or more persons in the Bible or if in your sermon a biblical person comes into your picture, consult *Who's Who in the Bible,* by Frank S. Mead, which I mentioned in the last chapter. His fine book has 250 short biographies. Each is a sort of snapshot picture of a person. It goes without saying that a good dictionary and a thesaurus are essential. A book of quotations, such as Bartlett's, and an encyclopedia of quotations will give your sermon added polish, color, and clarity. I have other books on my shelf, but their contribution to the preparation of a sermon has been less than 1 percent. To engage in deep and exhaustive reading is too time consuming and, in your early experiences, may prove confusing and/or discouraging.

While you have been reading, you have been taking notes and putting them into the picture pattern on the floor or on the wall. Having completed this step, now research your own thinking on the subject. Audibly talk to yourself about each of the notes. Move them from one place to another and make notes. Disagree with yourself on this or that. Anticipate. When I was learning to drive, my father said, "To be a safe driver, you must anticipate what might be around the curve: the child playing by the road or the car approaching from a side road." A good speaker or lecturer must anticipate the variety of people in his audience. Ask, "What unique connotations will this word or phrase have to my audience?" and "What kind of questions will this statement create?" Remember that a question mark is shaped like a hook, and a question can cause a listener to be "hooked" at the point in your sermon where it occurred.

At this point, you may want to put some of your notes in the file for another time. In all probability you have enough material for an hour and twenty minutes. This is something you could not believe would happen. So start rearranging your notes in some kind of sequence. The notes you remove, lay aside for now. When you get closer to the completion of your preparation, you may want one or more back in the picture.

You are now ready to develop the first picture of your sermon.

ASSEMBLY

At this point you have selected your topic, and you have collected a sizable amount of information that is in one way or another related to your topic. Two things must now be said. First, in no way consider that research is ended and "Assembly" has started. In spite of the "book mechanics," these two sections overlap considerably. While you are researching the subject, you are doing some assembly; and while you are assembling (putting it all together), you are going back for more research. Now that you are putting it together, you will be going back to the books and to your file.

The second thing that must be said is that at times when you reach this point, you will consider changing your subject. Don't. That is not to say that you should force it or try to bull your way through. The result will be disastrous because it will show that you don't have a good hold on your subject, but it is more difficult to find a new subject. The impulse to find a new topic tells you to go back and do more research. But stay with the subject.

Looking a little closer at what you now have, you will see that you have three things: (1) something that resembles a jigsaw puzzle, (2) puzzle parts that will be used in another sermon, and (3) the picture you have in your mind of what you want to put across. Those puzzle pieces on the floor will shortly become a picture. You must now begin your "weeding out." As was said before, eliminate from the bottom up. It is frequently difficult to decide which is the best: this or that? By eliminating from the bottom up, you are left with the best. What do you do with the weeds? Remember the words of Ralph Waldo Emerson who said, "And what is a weed? A plant whose virtues have not been discovered." So you put them back in your file.

In advertising, there are three commandments:

- Thou shalt stop the eye.
- Thou shalt deliver the message.
- Thou shalt make the sale.

You cannot do any less in your sermon. To stop the eye is to get the attention of the congregation. You probably have less than twenty seconds to get their attention. You may think that, by telling a few jokes, you will get the attention of the audience. My own opinion of jokes is that they are just candy. If you think that you must pass out candy to have your message accepted, then you don't have much to say. Confection for affection, it is called; but you are not there to make love. Candy decays teeth, and jokes decay sermons and speeches. Also, when you start to tell a joke right away, you may have ten people who have heard the joke, and they immediately turn to their neighbors and tell the punch line. It is nothing less than tragic when, as too often happens, persons stand in the pulpit and say that they themselves were participants in the joke, while one-fourth of the congregation has heard the story for years. Nothing can be said from that point to restore credibility. The benediction should follow immediately.

The real tragedy is that speakers try too hard to get attention. My formula is KISS, *Keep It Simple, Speaker*. For example, suppose that the passage of Scripture at the beginning of this chapter, Acts 28:3, caught your attention. If that were part of your sermon, don't you see how you can recall an outing or a church picnic and build your sermon from there? I recently heard the best baccalaureate sermon in my experience. Dr. Robert W. Neff began, "Twinkle, twinkle, little star; how I wonder. . . . Wonder, what a wonderful word." From where I was seated, I could see that he never lost the attention of one graduate. We have all gathered sticks; we have all said, "Twinkle, twinkle"; and we all have in common uncountable other things. So start on common ground, and in your message lift the audience to the level where you sell (make) your point.

First Outline Draft

You are now ready to draft your first outline. To say that an outline is important is to make an understatement. When you become reasonably well experienced, the preparation of a sermon may end with the second draft or first draft of your outline. Now, so I don't mislead you, the outline is like the skeleton or steel that gives bodies or buildings their strength and shape. The outline is, then, the framework of a sermon or a book. So master the ability to outline and learn to depend on it. If you don't remember how to outline, borrow a book on composition and turn to the section or chapter on outlines. Learn the basics of outlining. Learn the three kinds of outlines: topic, sentence, and paragraph. In preparing a sermon, you will start with a topic outline followed by a sentence outline.

Each and every time you write a sermon outline, put it to the test of these questions:
1. Does all the material bear upon the topic?
2. Does all the material treat a single subject?
3. Is the purpose of the material clearly visible?
4. What are the main points? What are the subordinate points?
5. What is the clearest and most effective argument?
At this point you may want to change or rearrange your outline. If you do, repeat the same test above.

Diagramming

In your high school English class you were probably taught not only to outline but also to diagram sentences. And, I suspect, your opinion of sentence diagramming was considerably lower than that of outlining. But diagrams are important to the skilled and can be

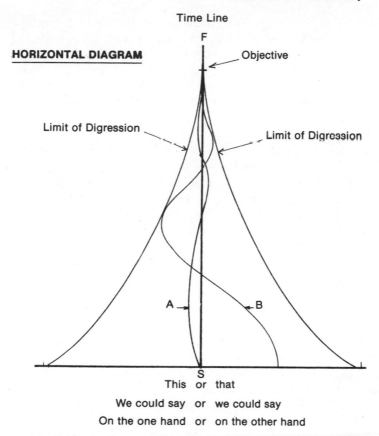

HORIZONTAL DIAGRAM

Time Line

F

Objective

Limit of Digression

Limit of Digression

A

B

S
This or that
We could say or we could say
On the one hand or on the other hand

very helpful to you. A sermon can be diagrammed in two ways. One way measures units left and right (the horizontal diagram) and the other up and down (the vertical diagram). For purpose of analyses, we can separate these two diagrams and study them one at a time. Therefore, let us look at the horizontal diagram first. Simply, the left and right, or horizontal diagram, is like footprints in sand or snow. In a sermon the horizontal diagram is the locus of points (line of footprints) leading from the starting point, S, the introduction, to the finish, F. From your outline you must decide if the horizontal diagram is a straight line from S to F or something else, perhaps a this-way and that-way random walk. Speakers who do the random walk make you wonder how they ever got to the conclusion. Then there are speakers whose diagram is a circle. They announce their conclusion at the beginning and spend twenty minutes justifying their conclusion. As you see, you may leave at any time. You are already convinced of their conclusion. This kind of speech may be identified as an "Indian war dance." Then there are the "ice skaters," so-called because of the tracks they make in the ice. They zig this way, zag that way, zig, zag, and, on the average, they get there. Unfortunately, each time they zig or zag—digress—some people keep on going and you have lost them. Just picture what happens when a speaker tells a short story of fishing in Canada. When the speaker returns to his topic, the fisherman keeps on fishing.

One technique for holding to your subject is to have a key word, phrase, or sentence; periodically in the course of your sermon repeat that word, phrase, or sentence. For example, you could choose the phrase "Twinkle, twinkle, little star; how I wonder. . . ," or "And he gathered a bundle of sticks and put them on the fire."

The vertical diagram is like a curve on graph paper representing a stock market report or rise in the cost of living. The starting point in the case of a sermon is not zero but at the level at which you and your listeners were when you came together. Give it an arbitrary value of, let us say, one on a scale of one to ten. So the starting point is one, and you hit the main sell, the climax, at ten. The time base is twenty minutes, and you should hit the level of ten about one or two minutes before the end of the twenty-minute period. What are the units of the one-to-ten vertical scale? The units are a combination of tempo, density of material, intensity of expression, and many more things. The curve should be a uniform rise—no humps or dips. After reaching the peak of ten, the drop-off should also be uniform, but not to less than seven. Obviously, these are not precisely measurable numbers. They are subjective. With some experience they are repeatable measurements.

More Rules

Well, it is time for more rules. The rules at this point are ones you have already thought of or recognized. The first rule is that you are there to *express,* not to *impress.* I am confident that to impress people has not been part of your plan. But the tendency can creep in, and you should bend over backward to avoid it. Not only should you speak to be understood, but you should also speak so that you are not misunderstood. Select words that are free of undesirable connotations. *Never talk down.* Avoid words or phrases that need explaining.

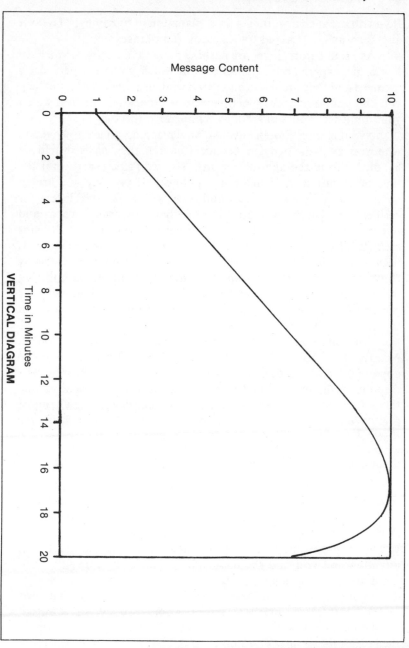

If you do use such a word, get an explanation in by saying, "To say it another way . . ."; avoid trade words and phrases.

As I said before, jokes are nothing more than candy. If you have humorous experiences or anecdotes in which you were personally involved and they are warm and wonderful, use them. They will help you and your audience. When you do tell this kind of story, watch your audience; you will see how many are with you.

Avoid clutter. Statements like how pleased you are to be there, who you are, and what a beautiful church they have should be handled during the announcements. You won't be charged for the time or attention. And make no apologies. If you say you are an inexperienced speaker, your audience will look and listen for verification. The worst clutter is those habit or crutch words and phrases. The most popular clutter now is "you know." Perhaps mention of this problem should have been made back in chapter 1, because crutches like this must be removed even from your everyday conversation. I regret to report hearing a minister with fifteen minutes of good sermon and five minutes of "you know's." The practice is not only annoying but is also a serious diluter, a thief of time.

There are many words and phrases that can get you in trouble. Nearly all of them you will recognize. There is one that is not so apparent: "You must agree." I know there are people like me who respond, "Oh, yeah?" but I think it is an instinctual reaction, and there are so many nicer ways to handle the matter. Some examples are: "Would you join me in saying . . .," "Don't you find it true that . . .," or "I will agree with you if you say. . . ."

Incubation

Now comes one of the most fascinating parts of preparing a sermon. The human mind has the capacity to work on a problem while you are talking or doing something else. Have you ever tried to think of a person's name and could not? Then, some time later, while you were doing something totally unrelated, the name flashed to your attention and you said the name aloud. This same capacity of the mind to search and to put ideas in place will work for you in developing a sermon, and this is the next step. Put everything away and forget it for one or, if you have the time, two days. The word is *incubation* and it works. It is like weight lifting: the more you do it, the greater the results. You won't forget what you have set aside time to think about. A relevant thought will pop into your mind and you will grab a scrap of paper, scribble a note, and put it with your last outline.

When you go back to work on the sermon, read your subject and objective and study your Scripture passage again. Take your outline and deliver a trial sermon, noting changes and additions as you go. When you have finished, talk to yourself about it and then write a new draft of the outline. You may decide at this point that you have what you want or that you wish to run it through another incubation.

Using a Tape Recorder

Some people think a tape recorder is useful in these practice sessions. I don't. I don't like my own picture (I am sure I am much better looking than the picture shows), and there is a funny noise in my microphone voice. The real problem with listening to yourself is that there is a tendency to become discouraged with your voice and your delivery. Part of the reason for this is that the condition of you and a recorder in a room with no time limit and freedom to start over in no way corresponds to the real conditions. The pitch and volume of voice will be different, and your timing will be so poor as to cause you almost to stutter. Later on in your experience as a lay preacher, record a practice session and then sneak a recorder into the pulpit and record the sermon as given. The difference will be more than you can believe.

Difficult Passages

Earlier I spoke of those special times when you decide to tackle a passage which you don't understand but which keeps haunting you. When you crack one of these, you've got a winner. You can tell of your search as if it were a detective story or a search for a long lost object. As soon as you attack the problem, keep a notebook log of everything that takes place. When you have solved it, condense the log into an outline in the same sequence. Include the blind alleys. This method has worked well for me and every similar sermon I have heard was just great. The first time I heard this done, the speaker's opening line went something like this: "I still don't know what I am going to talk about. I started reading on what I thought was going to be my subject and somehow I got on to . . .," and on he went. When he got finished, everyone was listening with rapt attention. You can't do it very often. But it works.

Your Pulpit Notes

After two, three, or four drafts of your sermon, you have decided that "This is it"; it's not perfect, you say, but you are ready to go with it. Don't try to achieve perfection, because no one is perfect. With a few mechanical adjustments you are ready to go.

For your speaking outline, fold in half two or three sheets of lightweight paper about eight by ten inches in size. Put them together like a small five- by eight-inch book, and number the pages by hand. Take the pages apart, and type or print your outline on the pages as they are numbered. When you reassemble the pages, you have a booklet of your sermon outline. Place your outline booklet in your Bible adjacent to your Scripture source. Now take a strong white thread and tie it there by passing it up the centerfold of the booklet, called the saddle, and down between the back and the binding of the Bible. Pull it tight and tie it. When you do this, it is there to stay—you won't lose it—and (a little untruth) it will appear that you are speaking right from the Bible. Now with a straight edge and two colored pencils run through your sermon and underline any part to which you want to give extra emphasis.

It seems to you now that I have put you through a lot of work. That is true, but let me say two things. As you develop as a lay preacher, you will omit some of these steps, and others you will do automatically. Second, let me tell you of an experience I had. My father had just finished demonstrating a machine he was selling. The man said, "It takes a long time to operate that machine." My father replied, "No, it always takes longer to tell how to do something than to do it." "I don't believe that," said the man. To which my father said, "How long does it take you to tell someone how to button a button?" With that he got the order.

I have a wish—a wish that I might be there and hear your first sermon. In prayer I will be, but I know that you will have much better company. God bless you, and may you pray not that you will deliver a good sermon, but that the people will hear a good sermon. God stands between your lips and their consciousness.

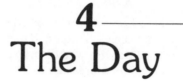

4
The Day

"So Paul stood up, and motioning with his hand said. . . ."   Acts 13:16

Today is the day and you ARE ready. Believe it because it is true. When it is over, you will know that you were ready. This is what should be in your mind when you get up in the morning. Since you are ready, go about getting up as though it were any similar morning. Have your shower and make any other preparation you usually do. Read the paper and have your breakfast. Do you think I am getting away from the subject? No, because as soon as you start doing unusual things, breaking your pattern, such as getting up earlier than usual or not reading the paper, you are out of contact, out of step with yourself, and things go from bad to worse. Don't even think about the service or the sermon. If you do, you will start asking yourself silly questions like, "Does the choir sing before or after the offering?" or, "I wonder if there is a better passage reference for the closing?" If you go over your sermon in detail, you will make a change. If you make a change, you will mess it up. I heard a high school football coach explain when asked why the team didn't pass; he said, "When you pass, three things can happen and two of them are bad news." There are three kinds of last-minute changes you can make and *all three* have bad results. You can change the order of things and destroy the continuity; you can add something, only to realize while you are preaching that it just doesn't fit; or you can remove something, only to create a big black hole in your sermon. Look at your sermon to see if the pages are all there and in the right order, just as you would make sure that your necktie is inside your vest or that your earrings match your dress, whichever the case may be.

APPEARANCE

You must give thought to how you dress. Whether you like it or not, you speak out before you open your mouth. If you step in the pulpit in a dress, suit, shirt, or necktie with wild colors, somebody is going to say, "Hey, we have a clown for a preacher today." I have seen people distracted when a minister in a white shirt and a dark gray suit wore white socks. I suppose one way of making my point is: Don't let your clothing outshout you. You are there to speak out for Jesus Christ, not your wardrobe.

Here is a touchy matter—beards. If you wear a beard that obscures your mouth visually, to many it will be obscured aurally. Visual contact with the mouth is an aid to aural communication. This is particularly true for those suffering hearing impairment in one or both ears. If you question this, have someone talk to you while holding a hand or card to block your view of his or her mouth. At first you will say it makes no difference. But as you become more interested in what they are saying, you will want the obstruction removed. By covering your mouth, you are giving up a communication link with your audience. You have noticed, I am sure, when watching a movie in the theater or on television, that music is used to set the mood of what is about to come. The facial expressions of an experienced speaker will do the same thing. For example, you will get twice the response to a funny story if you first light up with a smile than if you begin with a straight or somber face. With a full beard, it doesn't matter what kind of an expression you have. Some stories have a subtle humor to them, and your audience will wait for you to smile before they will.

ORGANIZATIONAL ARRANGEMENTS

Before this point in time, there are certain arrangements that must be agreed upon and people with whom you should touch base. Here is what you should do. First and foremost, are you going to be assisted in the pulpit, or are you to do the entire service? I can find no good reason for you to be assisted. The advantages to you and the good of the service are many if you lead from invocation to benediction. While you are leading the singing, making announcements, reading the Scriptures and the responsive reading, and bringing the morning prayer, you have no time to get more nervous. In fact, quite the opposite reaction takes place. You will become more relaxed. By the time you start your sermon, you have had an opportunity to learn how your audience responds. Your audience will know you better. After all, you have been talking to them and leading them for thirty-five minutes before your sermon. During the announcement time, you can make those nonsermon remarks. You can put your audience at ease. Make no apologies or excuses for being there, and make no plea for sympathy. After all, you are doing what you want to do; later you are going to feel good about what you have endeavored to do, so tell them you are glad to be there. It may sound a little trite, but that won't hurt, particularly if you can come up with a new way of saying it. "I have always wondered what it was like up here, and I am beginning to see that I am going to like it," is an example. Keep it brief, or the audience is going to suspect you are hiding something.

I have found it advantageous to meet with the choir director, the organist, and the head usher. The one time I didn't, the special music had been cancelled. I read the Scripture and sat down for the special music. Soon I realized that I was getting the "psst" signal. I looked at the choir and got no special music sign. Realizing that my sermon was not expandable, I selected a hymn and had the congregation sing an extra hymn. So, meet with the choir director, organist, and head usher. Ask if there is anything you should know. For example, should you give a signal for the choral response as you approach the end of the morning prayer? When do you pick up the offering plates—do the ushers hand them to you? Learn everything you can so that the service will go as smoothly and reverently as possible.

THE PUBLIC ADDRESS SYSTEM

The microphone could take a chapter of its own. But let me give you a short course on microphone systems (or public address systems) and what you should know about them. First of all, when I say "microphone" or "public address system," I am talking about the complete system. The microphone you use, the one at the choir, the amplifier, and the speakers are all part of the system. If you don't know, you should find out about the system you are using. Is the microphone directional? Is it on a stand or mounted? Is it on or do you switch it on? Does the amplifier have compression limiting, and where are all of the speakers? Now, let me go back over these questions.

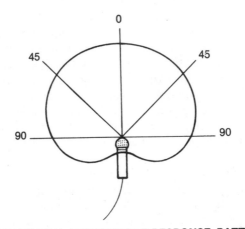

DIRECTIONAL MICROPHONE RESPONSE PATTERN

The response of a microphone itself is not the same in all directions or at all distances. All microphones are directional to one degree or another. Most microphones used in churches have what is called a cardioid or unidirectional pattern. That means that you get maximum response when you are talking straight into the end which is pointing at you. The response on the opposite end is virtually zero. The maximum response on your end holds for about twenty degrees to the right, left, above, and below center. To help you visualize that angle, go into your church some evening, take a square piece of paper, and fold it in half diagonally. Place one of the small angles under the microphone (or where it would be if you had a microphone) on the pulpit so that the extension of the two sides forming the angle go equally either side of you. The lines formed by these two sides are the equal volume limits where you can speak. If you move left or right beyond that angle to, say, twice the angle and the same distance from the microphone, your voice will only be one-fourth as loud. If you double the angle again, your voice will only be one-tenth as loud. That is what we mean by directivity.

Another property of the microphone that you need to know is called the "inverse square law." That simply means that if you are speaking one foot from the microphone and, for some reason, you step back one foot farther from the microphone, your voice will be one-fourth as loud as it was when you were one foot closer. So, with the directivity and inverse square law properties of microphones, pay attention to where you stand. It is possible to orient the microphone to make these properties offset one another. While standing close to the lectern, point the microphone down so that your voice is forty-five degrees above the microphone axis and therefore one-fourth the sensitivity. Then, when you step back, you will be inside the twenty-degree limit but one-fourth lower because of distance.

Some amplifiers have compression limiting. This means that if you were to shout or bend forward and talk right into the microphone, the compression limiting automatically turns the volume down for as long as necessary and then returns it to normal. This feature is nice because it spares people from being blasted out of their pews.

Except for the one minor adjustment described above, keep your hands off the microphone. If it is on a floor stand during the first hymn, see that it is not touching the lectern. Otherwise as you move the lectern with your hands or body, a banging noise will be heard on the speakers. If it is mounted to the lectern, then remember that anything hard, like belt buckles, rings, bracelets, and wristwatches, when striking wood will be heard very loudly on the speaker. No pounding, either!

You can take advantage of a microphone's properties in other ways. For example, move in close on the microphone for a loud whisper or if you want to do a short two-person dialogue. For person number one, speak in a normal voice in the normal place. For person number two, step around the side of the lectern and speak in a loud voice.

The microphone is here to stay. This we know and, therefore, it is important that you develop a style of speaking that is compatible with its properties. When speaking before a microphone in a church service, the volume will be set at a level so that the speaker can stand in a normal stance without bending over. You may turn your face left and right about thirty degrees without affecting the sound level. Beyond that angle, move your head to the opposite side so that your voice is projecting in the direction of the microphone. In other words, if you are going to face almost to your full right, then lean your body to the left and a little forward so that the microphone is nearly in line with the direction you are facing; watch a political speaker when he or she is in front of a microphone on a platform. This procedure is not necessary if there are two microphones about eighteen inches apart. Dual microphones give the speaker much more freedom.

During the singing of hymns, remember that your voice is going to be very loud on the speakers. At these times I recommend that, if you have the voice and experience to lead singing, by all means stand right up there and do it. However, be sure to sing all the verses. If you plan to drop out on the last verse to save your voice or to prepare for that which is to follow, step back from the microphone at the beginning. If you don't, and you stop singing, many will wonder why you did so. One step back should put your speaker voice equal to their voices. Two steps back (if you can't sing at all) will put your voice at a very low level.

DELIVERY

In public speaking courses two points are usually stressed. First, for a speech to be made, there are two important ingredients: a speaker and an audience. Both are your responsibility. Second, you have the responsibility to prepare the speech, and you have the responsibility of communicating that speech to your audience. To communicate your speech to your audience, you must gain and maintain their attention. To communicate, we employ what one writer calls metacommunication. Simply, whenever we communicate, we use the spoken language and body language—the aural and the visual.

In the three preceding chapters I have talked about finding what to say and then putting it together. Now you are going to say it to your audience. No matter how well you have selected your topic, researched the material, and organized your sermon, you can lose it all in the delivery. A sermon that was good as prepared can come out poor, fair, good, or very good, with all the grades in between. So when you observe ministers and others, give attention to those who communicate the best with you and others. Be careful, though; there are those who storm in a pulpit. They shout and put on all kinds of theatrics. The shouters don't have much to say. They are like a fast-ball pitcher; they are trying to blow it past you. One popular preacher once said of his pulpit efforts, "I always roar when I have nothing to say." Many are taken in by these acts, but time erases them and their effects. So when you observe a speaker, be sure that it is someone who has passed the test of time and results. Take notice of his or her aural and visual methods and practice them.

Your voice should be strong, not just to be heard but in order to reflect the strength of what you have to say. A weak voice makes a weak sermon. A strong voice, be it adult male or female, or a young person's, does not mean shouting. A strong voice builds confidence in yourself and your listeners. A strong voice will keep you from being nervous. So stand up and speak out. Jesus certainly had a strong voice because he spoke to "great crowds."

Someplace in my books on photography, there is a statement that goes like this: The way you walk, the way you swing your hips, or how you use your arms tell very little about you. What you are, what you feel, and what you want to communicate, are all carefully framed between your neck and your hairline. The expressions of your face can introduce what you are going to say next and can set a mood. So pause and smile just before you tell something humorous. Keep on smiling as you tell it. Look pained or distressed as you begin to paint a picture of sadness or distress. In short—act. Above all though, since you want everyone's attention, you must give them your attention. So look at your audience—the entire audience. Don't look off to one side and give some people the idea that someone is holding cue cards there for you to read. We see enough of that on television when some celebrity is giving a testimonial for a product. Your eye action should relate to your thought action. If you are explaining how you searched for this or that, then run your eyes over the congregation as though you were looking for someone with a purple necktie. If you are asking, "What kind of a letter of recommendation for Jesus Christ are you?" (2 Corinthians 3:1), don't just look at one spot in the audience and ask that question. The others will think, "Boy, I'm glad I'm not sitting over there!" Mentally divide the audience into four equal areas. Look at each of the four areas separately and ask the same question of each area. By so doing, you have the license to repeat the question, and you are making sure the people know you mean everyone.

Your eyes are one of the most important links between you and your audience. When you look people in the eyes, you are giving them the feeling of a person-to-person relationship. And, as described above, you can control their behavior.

Now, consider your hands. If you have ever had a good portrait photographer take a full-length seated picture of you, you may recall how particular he or she was about your hands. Do you know that there are professional models who get three to five hundred dollars per hour for their hands only? Not only do they have well-shaped hands, but they also know how to communicate with them. Remember this the next time you see advertisements for gloves, nail polish, or jewelry. If your hands are gripping the edges of the lectern so your knuckles are white, you are in trouble and your audience knows it. Also, don't play the "cool cat" with one hand in your pocket playing with keys or coins. Be free with your hands and slightly fluid. As far as hand gestures are concerned, keep them at an absolute minimum. Later, when you have had formal instruction in public speaking, you can use more hand gestures. My use of hand gestures is almost nil. So, for the present, keep your hands out of the action.

One habit speakers frequently have is that of shifting their weight from one foot to the other. As time goes on, the tempo increases until they look like they are doing the rumba. There are variations of this act, and they are all nervous outlets. Keep still. Men, if you are overweight around the belt, a good photographer will tell you to stand on one foot with the toe of the other just in back of the heel of the foot holding your weight. You will look thinner in that position. Don't put one foot so far back that it is vertical and then do a toe dance.

THE ORDER OF SERVICE

You may have attended one order of church service all of your life. But the first time you lead the services, you are going to need a bulletin. So take two into the pulpit. Put one on the pulpit and one on the table or chair beside you. If, before the service, you make a note in one, "do ye also the other."

In the front or back of nearly all hymnals there are printed selected invocations and benedictions. There are several in the back of this book. Find and mark them in advance of the service. Memorize one or two of each.

The morning prayer should be spontaneous and free of vain repetitions. Making it both spontaneous and delivered at a specific place in the program is difficult to do. To prepare a prayer to be read is possible, but such a prayer will be even further from genuine spontaneity. The best compromise is to work from an outline. Don't put it in with your sermon because you can use it every time you are to bring the morning prayer. In preparing the outline, for part of it consider the Lord's Prayer as a guide. After each use of an outline, improve it. After a time you won't need an outline.

AFTER THE SERMON

Now, after the closing hymn and the benediction, walk to the back of the church and begin receiving people as they leave the church. What do you say to each person? What you say is important but not critical. However, if you are a student of psychology, it can be a very interesting time, depending on who is in the congregation. There are some people who make a little intellectual fun game out of shaking hands in a line. They will throw a verbal ball at you, and you may not even know a game was on. Of the many stories I could tell, I'll give you one. A man who was very clearly in his nineties said, "You used the Revised Standard Translation, but I am old enough to know the King James is the one that is right." I replied, "I am amazed; I would not have guessed you were nearly that old." The twinkle in his eye gave him away. He replied, "You are OK; I hope you come back." He wanted to see if I was paying attention. You, too, must pay attention. Be courteous and remember what they say. If someone says something that sounds like an attack, you have misunderstood.

You will get compliments—some routine, some charitable, and some sincere. I don't think you ever learn how to sort them out. When someone says, "I enjoyed your sermon," unless you know the person, you could put his or her remark in any one of the three bins: good, better, or best. I have never given much attention to those who say, "You gave us something to think about." Do they mean something to think about in lieu of listening or that they must think about whether or not to invite me again? They mean well, though, so I am happy.

After most of the people have departed, someone usually will hand you an envelope. It will be a check for the supply and travel expenses. What do you do with it? You accept the check and repel any thought to do otherwise. Here is why:

1. There were others before you who accepted the money, and others will follow who will accept the money. If you refuse, you are making a commentary on them.

2. Churches budget money for supply preaching. If you refuse and you do this for three, four, or five times, you upset the next year's budget because budgets are usually based on 90 percent last year's experience and 10 percent hope.

3. If you refuse and are invited back, you just may have bought
   your return.
4. If you refuse the payment and they really liked your sermon,
   they may not invite you back, not wanting to take advantage
   of your generosity.

What you do with the money is up to you. If it bothers you, cash
the check and put it in the collection at the next place you supply. If
you are a frequent speaker at some church other than your own, wait,
and when they have some special fund drive, return it then. When I
started, my library of books that would aid me was nil. So some of the
money I received went for books and will continue to do so.

5

What Next?

"Do not judge by appearances, but judge with right judgment." (John 7:24)

As you have heard it said (and it is always true), there are three speeches: the one you planned, the one you gave, and the one you wish you had given. As for sermons, there is a fourth: the one they heard and witnessed. Time will only tell you a part of what that fourth sermon was.

Your work is not finished. As soon as possible after the sermon, sit down alone and in a quiet place, and, as objectively as you can, analyze what took place. Don't be negatively critical of your performance, and don't be generous. Write down any thoughts you have at that moment. Recalling the guidance given in the preceding chapters, write the answers to these questions about your performance:

1. Aside from more practice, what must I do further to prepare myself as a lay preacher?
2. Did I adequately research my subject?
3. Was my outline plan good? Was it well structured? Did it have continuity and uniform timing?

4. How did I present myself? Were my movements and stance well controlled?

5. Did I speak with clarity and strength?

With these same questions, go to someone who was present and who will give you reasonably objective answers. I would suggest (in this order) persons such as your pastor, the chairman of the deacon board, an English teacher, a personnel manager, a business executive, or anyone practiced in observing people. You will learn more if you ask them in advance to observe and make notes.

After your first sermon and on beyond your one hundredth, you are going to receive belated comments. They are wonderful—all of them—especially the ones which go like this, "I liked your sermon last Sunday, but I disagree with you on the point where you said. . . ." That person didn't just *listen*. He or she gave what you said his or her undivided attention. The disagreement means that this person measured and weighed what you said. You should feel indebted to people like this because your sermons after that time will be a measure better. You will remember that person the next time you prepare a sermon. In fact, you will be inclined to address several lines in his or her direction. But be subtle about it.

You will, as the last threads of nervousness wear off, feel pride in what you have done. That is good, but keep it inside. No matter how many sermons you have preached, wait until you have preached one hundred more before expressing your pride.

At this point go back and observe experienced ministers and speakers, now with a greater insight and more analytically. You will pick up pluses, minuses, and techniques not observed before. Watching speakers and watching their audiences will soon become a hobby. Excuse this analogy, but at times it is more fun watching the people than watching the monkeys at the zoo. If you get the opportunity, watch a real "pro" work an audience. As President Truman said, "Sometimes silence hits harder than words." A *little* acting adds flavor and spark to a sermon. One of my favorite preachers said, "Just for a moment I am not going to speak as a minister but person to person"; at which point he took off his robe and tossed it on his chair. After making that point, he put it back on.

You should extend your reading and study of theologically oriented books. You may want to purchase a few. In general, save your money for reference-type books. Discuss with your pastor various books you have or are planning to read. As your library builds, you can exchange books back and forth with him or her. After you both have read each book, discuss your individual reactions. With a little disagreement you will help each other.

I can only assume one thing now: you are going on with your plan to be a lay preacher. So, when you remove your sermon outline from your Bible, staple it along the centerfold or stitch it on a sewing machine. Be sure to put the date and place on the back. Also write a few lines or paragraphs so that if some day you get a short notice or want to do this sermon again at another place, you can do so. Expand your "thought and clipping file." Have one file where you will place sermon ideas and thoughts that you have put down on a particular subject along with its objective and Scripture references.

If you haven't already, consider joining a Toastmaster's Club and/or enrolling in a night school class on public speaking.

6

The Prayer Breakfast and Other Special Messages

Jesus said to them, "Come and have breakfast."
John 21:12

In chapter 1 I said that this book was not limited to help in preparing sermons to be delivered in church services. As you will see shortly, it is not; in this chapter I will discuss Christian messages that are not given in a Sunday morning church service. I know that you know that there are such times and places, but I wonder if you have stopped to think how many and how varied they are. The variety of times and places where a Christian message can be given is too great to be known. Suffice it to say that message opportunities extend from a fifteen-minute message at a prayer breakfast to one sentence or phrase at a business meeting.

Before getting into the specifics of special Christian messages, I think it is important to identify how they are different from a church sermon and how they are not different. The differences are physical, emotional, and contextual. Unchanged is the word of God and your determination to communicate that word. Also unchanged is most of the preparation described earlier in this book.

GENERAL DIFFERENCES

Since, in the case of a special message, you are not in a church sanctuary on a Sunday morning, your message should not sound "preachy"; rather it should sound "todayish." After all, on a Sunday morning the people arrive with the full knowledge and understanding that it is Sunday, they are in a church sanctuary, and a sermon will be "preached." Furthermore, by the time the sermon begins, there have been hymns, special music, Bible reading, and an offering. Everything has been done to create a spiritual couch. True, some are thinking of the golf game in the afternoon or boating, but those things put them in a positive mood. The advantage of the printed church bulletin should not be underestimated, and the Sunday-to-Sunday format removes any premature resistance. You do not have these aids when delivering a special message.

Earlier I said that a sermon is based on a passage of Scripture. That is, you speak from the Bible and relate it to now. A special message will be more effective if you take today's common experiences and problems and relate them back to the Bible. In other words, relate from now to the Bible or connect today and the Bible. Please note that I said *common* experiences. Don't try to extrapolate a unique experience of your own into a lesson for humankind.

In a church service, probably 90 percent of the people before you are members of that church. The remaining 10 percent know that they are in a church of that denomination. Elsewhere, they belong to this church, that church, or no church. After you have thought on this last point, think of Jesus facing the Jews, Pharisees, Sadducees, and Gentiles, not people of one mind but bound in different directions.

Selecting a subject or topic for a special meeting is easier because whatever brings these people together is a clue to selecting a topic. Later, when I give a few examples, you will see what I mean. As you become more practiced, you will find times when you can take a sermon you have delivered and rework it into a special message. It will take about two hours to rewrite.

When you are putting it together, you will use the same techniques as described earlier, except that your "objective" is now a Bible passage.

PRAYER BREAKFASTS AND OTHER ORGANIZATIONAL MEETINGS

To me, bringing the devotional message at a prayer breakfast requires more skill and steadfastness than preaching a sermon. The competition for the attention of your audience makes it difficult to be even moderately successful. The prologue of hymns in the church is replaced with getting up earlier than usual, ham, eggs, coffee, and diverse conversation. When you wrench most of the assembled from their second cup of coffee, some will give you their attention while the attention of others will flee to their jobs and a budget meeting, salary review, or material shrinkage meeting. I have never made a study to determine which ones fall into the latter group, but have theorized it is those who, at that point, look at their watches.

Earlier in this book I gave examples of how to select a topic. I am going to do it again, but this time I am going to show how that which the group has in common can be a guide to topic selection. Consider a group of business people.

1. Business people are concerned with marketing surveys and new business adventures. Well, wasn't the spying expedition into the Promised Land (Numbers 13:17-33) just such an inquiry? There was a majority report and a minority report. Some saw the dangers, others the opportunities.

2. Business people are interested in results. The parable of the three servants—to one the master entrusted five talents; another, two, and another, one, to each according to his ability. The parable first recognizes that people are different in their abilities. But even if a person's ability is a "one" rating, he or she must produce.

3. Foremen frequently cry that they need more people in their crew. But look at the story of Gideon (Judges 7) who learned that with three hundred soldiers (not thirty-two thousand), some ingenuity, and trust in the Lord, success was theirs.

If the group consists of an organization like the Boy Scouts, Jaycees, or Garden Club, obtain a copy of its creed or law and show how it not only agrees with Scripture, but also is supported and amplified by it. For example:

1. **Boy Scouts**—From the Boy Scout's manual you can get the Scout oath and tie it in with some passage of Scripture like 1 Timothy 4:6-10, or consider the twelve points of the Scout law.

2. **Jaycees** (Junior Chamber of Commerce)—They have a creed. It has six points relating to God, Brotherhood of Man, Justice, Government, Creation, and Service to Humanity. No

ten speakers can emerge with the same Bible reference.

3. **Garden Club**—You will need help from your pastor's library for this one. How many plants are spoken of in the Bible? There are the lilies (Matthew 6:28), the rose of Sharon (Song of Solomon 2:1)—was it a rose?—and the shrub from which the crown of thorns was made.

4. **Camping and Hiking Groups**—If they hold their meetings on a hillside, by a lake (sea), or on the bank of a river, make use of the fact that those are the places where Jesus conducted most of his ministry.

Let me say just a few words on some other groups. If you have an assembly of political figures, be aware that there are many political figures in the Bible. Nicodemus is one whom I have thought of most in this connection. While sitting on the supreme council of the Sanhedrin (John 3:1-21; 7:50-52 and 19:39), he felt the struggle in his heart between his responsibilities as a leader of the Jews and his respect and love for Jesus Christ.

A group of lawyers may want to hear an analysis of the legality of the trial of Jesus. Several treatments of his trial are now classics. You may obtain copies of them from the Masonic Service Association, Silver Spring, MD 20910.

So you see, when I say that the orientation of a prayer breakfast message is from today to the Bible, it is just that. You search for a topic not in the *Bible,* but rather in that which brings a particular group of people together. So remember, the orientation of your message at a prayer breakfast must be toward the common denominator of your audience.

Now, consider the possibility that you are called on to make a speech for an occasion not religious or prayer related. You prepare your speech, perhaps employing mechanics described earlier in this book, and you decide to flavor it with quotations. Every book of quotations which I know of includes quotations from the Bible. Therefore, you should not hesitate to use Bible quotations in a secular speech. On the contrary, you, as a lay speaker for the Lord, should prefer Bible quotations. If you are known as a lay speaker, the absence of biblical quotations can be very conspicuous.

SPOT SERMONS

Before concluding this chapter and the book, I will add a few brief words about "spot sermons." First, they are not extemporaneous sermons because they are as short as the word "spot" connotes. The average length of an effective spot sermon is probably about one sentence. It never occurs in the context of a worship service sermon or the message at a prayer breakfast. It is rarely, if ever, called a sermon. However, spot sermons can and do have greater impact and results than many twenty-minute sermons.

My selection for the greatest spot sermon is the response that Jesus made to those who brought before him the woman taken in adultery (John 8:3-11): "Let him who is without sin among you be the first to throw a stone at her." He didn't say, "It is written. . . ." He didn't even look at them but just wrote in the sand. They left and, by leaving, confessed not only their own sinfulness and guilt but also that Jesus had the authority to impose the restriction as to who could or could not throw the first stone. Everyone walked away. Everyone responded to that spot sermon.

The New Testament is filled with spot sermons. With but a few exceptions, the entire ministry of Jesus Christ was by way of spot sermons. When challenged by the Pharisees, he replied with short, mind-jabbing "spot sermons." With the exception of the Sermon on the Mount (beginning with Matthew 5) and the farewell discourse by Jesus (John 13:31-16:33), the sayings of Jesus that are recorded for us are so short that they are read in their entirety as the Scripture reading in a worship service. Is there, then, any question as to the importance of spot sermons?

The only preparation for spot sermons is to commit yourself to the following:

1. When the opportunity presents itself, you will speak if and only if you have something to say. Don't speak for the sake of being heard or identified. Actually, this should be every mature Christian's commitment.

2. Keep what you say light and soft. For example, you find yourself in a situation where company politics is running rampant. You have an opening to make a comment. You can say one of the following:

    (a) "It says in the Bible, James 3:16, 'For where jealousy and selfish ambition exist, there will be disorder and every vile practice.'" That is very authoritative and prompts such thinking as, "Oh, one of those," or "Who is he trying to impress?"

    (b) You omit the "James 3:16" and just say, "The Bible

says, 'For where. . . .'" This makes it a *little* more palatable.

(c) The most effective technique is to say something like, "This situation reminds me of something I read somewhere in the Bible," and then paraphrase James 3:16.

If you do the latter, someone is likely to ask where in the Bible that is found. At this point you take this person aside to your desk or to where you have a Bible, find the verse, and read it to him or her. After adding a few comments, return to what you were doing. *Don't try to inflate the opportunity.*

To me, and I don't think I am alone on this point, if someone spits out a passage of the Bible verbatim with the book, chapter, and verse, I question whether the person believes it, and I am fearful that another verbatim quote will follow. If the passage is given in his or her own words, I am convinced the passage is part of them.

You do not *select* a topic in a spot sermon because events, situations, and possibly material things will dictate what you can or cannot say. There is no research because there is not the time for it. So prepare for these opportunities. Read. Read the Bible, and as you do, think of the variety of applications to today's living which the passage you are reading includes. Imagine yourself in a variety of situations and, out loud, say what you would have said had you been in that situation. If you hear of an event that possibly would have been a place for a spot sermon, consider what you would have said had you been there. Remember, though, that rear-view mirrors have built-in visual correction to 20-20.

There is no real conclusion to this book and, I pray, none to your desire to speak up for the Lord. I close with my choice of a benediction:

"May the God of peace himself sanctify you wholly; and may your spirit and soul and body be kept sound and blameless at the coming of our Lord Jesus Christ. He who calls you is faithful, and he will do it" (1 Thessalonians 5:23, 24).

Appendix

Opening Readings and Benedictions

OPENING READINGS

The earth is the LORD's and
    the fulness thereof,
    the world and those who dwell therein;
for he has founded it upon the seas,
    and established it upon the rivers.

Psalm 24:1-2

Who shall ascend the hill of the LORD?
    And who shall stand in his holy place?
He who has clean hands and a pure heart,
    who does not lift up his soul to
        what is false,
    and does not swear deceitfully.

Psalm 24:3-4

O come, let us sing to the LORD;
    let us make a joyful noise to the
        rock of our salvation!

Let us come into his presence with
    thanksgiving;
  let us make a joyful noise to him
    with songs of praise!
For the LORD is a great God,
  and a great King above all gods.
Psalm 95:1-3

Serve the LORD with gladness!
  Come into his presence with singing!

Enter his gates with thanksgiving,
  and his courts with praise!
  Give thanks to him, bless his name!

For the LORD is good;
  his steadfast love endures for ever,
  and his faithfulness to all generations.
Psalm 100:2, 4, 5

O give thanks to the LORD, for he is good;
  his steadfast love endures for ever!
Psalm 118:1

This is the day which the LORD has made;
  let us rejoice and be glad in it.
Psalm 118:24

I lift up my eyes to the hills.
  From whence does my help come?
My help comes from the LORD,
  who made heaven and earth.
Psalm 121:1-2

Unless the LORD builds the house,
  those who build it labor in vain.
Unless the LORD watches over the city,
  the watchman stays awake in vain.
Psalm 127:1

Behold, how good and pleasant it is
  when brothers dwell in unity!
It is like the precious oil upon the
    head,
  running down upon the beard,
upon the beard of Aaron,
  running down on the collar of his
    robes!
It is like the dew of Hermon,
  which falls on the mountains of
    Zion!
For there the LORD has commanded
    the blessing,
  life for evermore.

Psalm 133:1-3

The LORD is near to all who call upon
    him,
  to all who call upon him in truth.
He fulfils the desire of all who fear
    him,
  he also hears their cry, and saves
    them.

Psalm 145:18-19

"Seek the LORD while he may be found,
  call upon him while he is near;
let the wicked forsake his way,
  and the unrighteous man his thoughts;
let him return to the LORD, that he
    may have mercy on him,
  and to our God, for he will
    abundantly pardon."

Isaiah 55:6-7

"But the hour is coming, and now is, when the true worshipers will
worship the Father in spirit and truth, for such the Father seeks to
worship him. God is spirit, and those who worship him must worship
in spirit and truth." John 4:23, 24

BENEDICTIONS

"The Lord bless you and keep you: The Lord make his face to shine upon you, and be gracious to you: The Lord lift up his countenance upon you, and give you peace." Numbers 6:24-26

May the God of hope fill you with all joy and peace in believing, so that by the power of the Holy Spirit you may abound in hope. Romans 15:13

The grace of the Lord Jesus Christ and the love of God and the fellowship of the Holy Spirit be with you all. 2 Corinthians 13:14

May the God of peace himself sanctify you wholly; and may your spirit and soul and body be kept sound and blameless at the coming of our Lord Jesus Christ. 1 Thessalonians 5:23

Now may the Lord of peace himself give you peace at all times in all ways. The Lord be with you all. 2 Thessalonians 3:16

May grace and peace be multiplied to you in the knowledge of God and of Jesus our Lord. 2 Peter 1:2